WORLD'S GREATEST ATHLETES

Tiger WOODS

By Bob Woods

The
Child's World
www.childsworld.com

Published in the United States of America by The Child's World®
1980 Lookout Drive • Mankato, MN 56003-1705
800-599-READ • www.childsworld.com

ACKNOWLEDGMENTS

The Child's World®: Mary Berendes, Publishing Director

Produced by Shoreline Publishing Group LLC
President / Editorial Director: James Buckley, Jr.
Designer: Tom Carling, carlingdesign.com
Assistant Editor: Jim Gigliotti

Photo Credits: Joe Robbins
Interior: All images courtesy Getty Images except 18, 21, 22, 25:
AP/Wide World; 3, 5: Joe Robbins.

LIBRARY OF CONGRESS
CATALOGING-IN-PUBLICATION DATA

Woods, Bob.
  Tiger Woods / by Bob Woods.
      p. cm. — (The world's greatest athletes)
  Includes index.
  ISBN 978-1-59296-884-8 (library bound : alk. paper)
  1. Woods, Tiger. 2. Golfers—United States—Biography. I.
Title. II. Series.

  GV964.W66W65 2008
  796.352092—dc22
  [B]

                                        2007032001

CONTENTS

It's Official: Tiger's Grrreat!

TIGER WOODS MAY OR MAY NOT MUNCH ON sugar-frosted flakes for breakfast, but this much we know for sure: Morning, noon, or night, he most definitely is one of the greatest golfers ever. That's a mouthful to say about an **ancient** sport that features a long list of past and present greats, such as Bobby Jones, Ben Hogan, Arnold Palmer, Jack Nicklaus, Lee Trevino, Greg Norman, Vijay Singh, and Phil Mickelson. Yet Tiger's tale, almost since he was born, has been extra-special.

Consider how much Tiger accomplished in his first 10 years as a **professional** golfer, beginning in 1996, when he was 20 years old:

• He won 77 tournaments, including 56 on the Professional Golfers Association (PGA) Tour.

• He won 13 "major" tournaments—the four most **prestigious** events held annually on the PGA Tour (the Masters, U.S. Open, British Open, and PGA Championship).

• He was selected as the PGA's Player of the Year a record eight times, and he was ranked the No. 1 golfer in the world eight years.

• He has earned a record total of more than $65 million in official prize money in his career.

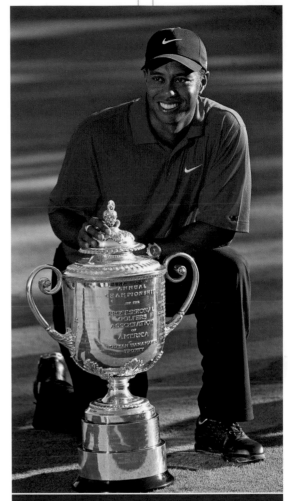

Tiger has won more events on the PGA Tour than any other active player.

Tiger first swung a golf club when he was 11 months old. He won his first tournament when he was eight. He claimed victory in three straight U.S. **Amateur** Championships and won an NCAA championship in college. And he accomplished more in the first decade of his pro career than all but a select few golfers in history. So it is not far-fetched to say that Tiger is well on his way to becoming the grrreatest golfer of all time.

CHAPTER 1

Born to be a Golfer

TIGER'S FATHER, EARL WOODS, WAS 42 YEARS OLD when he learned how to play golf. He was a retired lieutenant colonel and former Green Beret in the U.S. Army. He quickly fell in love with the game where you whack a little white ball with a long, clubbed stick. Not long after he and his second wife, Kultida, had a son in 1975, Earl decided he could teach the little guy to become a golfer, too—a really good golfer.

Eldrick Woods was born on December 30, 1975, in Cypress, California, a sunny suburb of Los Angeles, where people play golf year round. Before he was a year old, he was imitating Pop by swinging his golf clubs and hitting balls into a net. He started taking lessons when he was four, and he got his first set of clubs when he was five.

Earl Woods (left) took up golf after retiring from the U.S. Army. He passed along his passion for the game to Tiger.

By then, no one called the youngster Eldrick. Back when Earl was stationed in Vietnam, he had an Army buddy whom he called "Tiger" because he was so brave. Earl gave his baby boy the same nickname, hoping that someday "my son would be as courageous as my friend."

Young Tiger Woods showed no fear on the golf course, where he spent almost all of his spare time. "I played a whole bunch of other sports, and enjoyed them all," Tiger remembers, "but for some strange reason I just couldn't get away from golf. I loved it too much."

The reason wasn't strange at all. He simply was so much better than everyone else his age. He not only beat all of the local kids, but also young players from all over the world. Tiger won the Junior World Golf Championships an incredible six times—at ages 8, 9, 12, 13, 14, and 15!

Tiger helped Stanford win a national title in 1996, the same year that he won his third consecutive U.S. Amateur.

In 1991, also at 15, Tiger became the youngest winner ever of the U.S. Junior Amateur Championship. He captured that title again the following year, making history as the first back-to-back winner. He won it a third straight year in 1993.

The golfing **phenomenon** excelled off the course, as well. Tiger was an "A" student at Western High School in nearby Anaheim, California, then went on to study economics at Stanford University in Palo Alto, California. Naturally, he was the star of Stanford's golf team, which won the college national championship in 1996, Tiger's second year.

Meanwhile, Tiger continued to dominate in amateur golf tournaments. He triumphed in a trio of U.S. Amateur Championships, from 1994 to 1996—another spectacular feat that no one had ever done before. "That's a feeling I'll remember for the rest of my life," said a smiling Tiger after the '96 event, during which he staged an amazing rally to pull out a thrilling win. The match attracted a huge national TV audience, giving millions of future Tiger fans their first glimpse of the rising superstar.

One part of Tiger's story has nothing to do with how he hits the ball off the tee farther than most

Tiger has won 13 "majors" entering 2008. His ultimate goal is to overtake the legendary Jack Nicklaus' record total of 18 major championships.

players. Nor is it about his superior "short game"— golf lingo for how he well he plays when the ball is near or on the green. Rather, the other part of his story is the biological fact that he is, as he likes the say, "Cablinasian." That's Tiger's made-up word to

He looks so young! Tiger was only 14 when he posed with his dad and his mom in this photograph from 1990.

Young Tiger Woods

> When he was just two years old, Tiger appeared on TV's *Mike Douglas Show*. Besides showing off a pint-size swing many adults wish they had, the phenom had a putting contest with the late comedian Bob Hope. He wowed viewers again at age 5 when he was featured on *That's Incredible*.

> At age 8, Tiger played in the Junior World Championship for the first time. The tournament was held at the Presidio Hills Golf Course in San Diego. Competing against golfers 10 and under, Tiger won by shooting a five-under-par final round. He went on to win the annual event five more times.

> Winning his third straight U.S. Amateur Championship—which no one had done before—was no easy feat for 20-year-old Tiger. As the final round began, he was losing to Steve Scott. Tiger battled back all day, finally tying Scott on the 17th hole and forcing a playoff. On the second hole, Tiger tapped in an 18-inch putt to take the lead—and make golf history. "This is by far the best," Tiger said. "It's just an unbelievable feeling."

describe his **diverse ethnicity**. Earl was African-American, Native-American, and Chinese. Kultida is from the southeast Asian country of Thailand. So Tiger's Caucasian, black, American Indian, and Asian.

Regardless of his family's past, present-day Tiger was ready to rock the golf world when he became a professional on the PGA Tour in the summer of 1996.

CHAPTER 2

Welcome to "Tigermania"

MOST COLLEGE STUDENTS WORRY ABOUT GETTING good grades, making it to classes on time, and having fun on the weekends. That's what life was like for Tiger at Stanford. Unlike his classmates, though, he also was under incredible pressure to become a professional golfer. He already was the most successful amateur player in the history of the sport, so fans wondered, why shouldn't he graduate to the PGA Tour and earn money for his victories?

Actually, Tiger played in his first PGA tournament, the Nissan Los Angeles Open, in 1992, though he could not collect any money for it. At 16 years and two months old, he became the youngest golfer ever to compete in a PGA Tour event. He kept up with older and more experienced pros the first

At 16, Tiger already was competing with the big boys. He played in the Nissan Open in Los Angeles in 1992.

day (most men's tournaments are four days long, usually Thursday through Sunday, with 18 holes played each day), but failed to make the "cut" (after

In His Own Words

On balancing golf and school as a kid growing up in California:

"I always wanted to play in every tournament there was. Realistically, that wasn't possible. So my parents had to keep a close eye on that and always stress the schoolwork first. My mom always used to tell me that if I didn't have my homework done, I couldn't go practice. And, yeah, that happened lots of times."

On his trademark fist pump when he makes a tough shot in a close match:

"It's like a football player catching a pass, running in for a touchdown, and spiking the ball. I don't think that's rubbing it in. You've just accomplished something."

On remembering his father, Earl Woods, who passed away on May 3, 2006:

"My dad was my best friend and greatest role model, and I will miss him deeply. He was an amazing dad, coach, mentor, soldier, husband, and friend. I wouldn't be where I am today without him."

the second day, if a player doesn't achieve a certain score, he doesn't qualify for weekend play). "I think these were the best two days of my life," Tiger said after Friday's round. His words were sincere, though Tiger and the other golfers knew that even better days lay ahead. "I've got a lot of growing to do, both physically and mentally," the teenager added, "but I'll play these guys again—eventually."

The following year, Tiger played in three PGA tournaments. Unfortunately, he missed the cut in all three. It was the same in 1994. Then he was invited to participate in the 1995 Masters, the famous

Tiger is a perfectionist who has always tried to make his swing even better.

tournament played every April at the Augusta National Golf Club in Georgia. Tiger made the cut, but finished tied for 41st place. Regardless, the 19-year-old made plenty of great shots, impressed his fellow golfers, and remained confident in his abilities. Looking at a wall of photos of past

Tiger won for the first time on tour in this tournament in Las Vegas in 1996.

Masters champions, Tiger boldly predicted, "Someday, I'm going to get my picture up there."

It wouldn't be long. A few days after his historic third consecutive U.S. Amateur win, Tiger left Stanford and turned pro in August 1996. The excitement the 20-year-old generated became known as "Tigermania." The buzz was not only because he'd shown such awesome potential to become a superstar pro, but also because there have been so few African-Americans on the PGA Tour. Many people expected Tiger to inspire young blacks to take up golf.

Even before he took his first swing as a pro, Tiger became a rich young man. As an amateur athlete, he could not receive payment as a spokesperson for a company's products. But when he turned pro, Tiger immediately signed a

Scoring in Golf

In golf, the lowest score wins. Each hole is given a "par"—which is the number of shots, or strokes, it takes to get the ball from the tee to the hole—varying between three, four, or five. Most 18-hole courses average out to par 72. If a player goes two strokes under par on any single hole, it's scored an "eagle." One under par is a "birdie." One over par is a "bogey." Two over is a "double bogey," and so on. (Some events, such as at Las Vegas, are five-day events. If a player shot par there, it was scored 360.)

five-year contract with Nike worth $40 million, and another five-year deal, for $20 million, with Titleist (a maker of golf balls and clubs).

In his first few months on the PGA Tour, Tiger proved that he definitely belonged. He won two tournaments, including the Las Vegas Invitational. In that one, he shot a remarkable 27 strokes under par.

Tiger finished '96 with high honors. He was named the PGA Rookie of the Year and *Sports Illustrated*'s Sportsman of the Year. SI's cover story, "The Chosen One," praised Tiger as "the rare athlete to establish himself immediately as the dominant figure in his sport." Tigermania, however, was just getting started.

Yeaaaah! Tiger's fist pump here came after he sank the putt to win the Masters for the fourth time in his career in 2005.

CHAPTER 3

Master of the Golf Universe

IN 1997, HIS FIRST FULL YEAR ON THE TOUR, Tiger got off to a roaring start. In January, he won the season-opening Mercedes Championships tournament, although it wasn't easy. On the final day, he finished tied with 1996 Player of the Year Tom Lehman, which forced a **sudden-death playoff**. On the first hole, Tiger nailed a dramatic birdie to seal the deal.

Tiger was just getting warmed up. At the Masters in April, he entered another zone—and the record books at Augusta National.

The Masters is to golf what the Super Bowl is to football. It's the Big One that every PGA golfer wants to win at least once in his career. The four-day annual tournament is played on a lush green golf course that was founded by golf legend Bobby Jones in 1933. Its fairways are lined with tall trees and bright red, purple, and white azalea bushes. Yes, Augusta is beautiful, but its 18-hole, par-72 course is also one of the toughest tests for even the most experienced pros.

So here comes Tiger in 1997, only 21 years old and playing in his very first major tournament as a pro. By the end of the first day, Thursday, the new kid on the **links** proved he was the man to beat. He was lousy on the first nine holes, shooting a disastrous 40, including four bogeys. Then, on the back nine, Tiger adjusted his swing and shot an amazing 30. His final score of 70 left him three shots behind the day's leader.

Tiger blew away the competition on each of the next three rounds. He had the day's lowest score, 66, on Friday and led by three shots. On Saturday, he tripled his lead to nine with a jaw-dropping 65. Sunday, wearing his **signature** red shirt—Tiger wears red every Sunday during tournaments—he cruised to his first major title with a three-under-par 69.

When Tiger slipped on the traditional green sports jacket, the "trophy" that every Masters winner

> Tiger Woods is a household name—and not just among golfers. He's often seen in television commercials for several big companies.

receives—he held a string of records to go with it. His total score of 270—18 shots under par—broke a 32-year-old Masters record set by six-time winner Jack Nicklaus. Tiger's 12-shot lead over 47-year-old runner-up Tom Kite was the largest margin of victory in Masters history. And Tiger became the youngest-ever Masters champ. With 40 million TV viewers watching in awe, he set a total of 20 Masters records and tied six others.

The previous Masters winner (Vijay Singh here) always puts the green jacket on the current winner (Tiger in 2001).

Perhaps more significantly, Tiger became the first African-American winner at Augusta National—a golf club that hadn't accepted black members until six years earlier. In fact, Tiger was the first black golfer to win any major. What's more, his historic moment came 50 years after Jackie Robinson became

Augusta National is one of golf's most beautiful settings—but for a long time the club excluded African-Americans.

the first African-American allowed to play Major League Baseball. "Tiger Woods isn't like any other golfer," said Lee Elder, who was the first black golfer to play in the Masters, in 1975. "Him winning this major event like this, I think it's just like what Jackie Robinson did."

Fast-forward a decade to the 2007 Masters, at which Tiger finished tied for second. By then, he'd put on the green jacket three more times: in 2001, 2002, and 2005.

In 2001, Tiger finished at 16 under par, beating David Duval by two strokes. With his second Masters win, Tiger became the first golfer ever to hold all four major titles at once. After finishing fifth in the 2000 Masters, he had gone on to win that year's other three majors—the U.S. Open, the British Open, and the PGA Championship.

"It's hard to believe," he said, "because there are so many things that go into winning a major championship. You've got to have some luck. You have to get some breaks. You have to have everything go right. To have it go right four straight times, some of the golf gods are looking on me the right way." And they haven't turned away since.

CHAPTER 4

The Greatest Golfer Ever?

A FAVORITE **PASTIME** FOR FANS OF ANY SPORT IS debating who was, or is, the greatest ever. In baseball, many say it's Babe Ruth. Lots of NFL fans say Jim Brown was the best running back ever, while today Peyton Manning gets plenty of votes for greatest quarterback of all time. In hockey, few argue against Wayne "The Great One" Gretzky, while in basketball, Michael Jordan is generally considered the best ever.

When he was a teenager and winning every amateur championship on the planet, experts were already predicting that Tiger Woods had a chance to be golf's greatest player ever.

During the first 11 years of his professional career, Tiger certainly lived up to those high expectations for golfing success.

Tiger is probably the most skilled player on tour. It is his focus and determination, however, that really sets him apart.

While a golfer's performance in the four majors is the best measuring stick, how he does in other tournaments counts, too. Consider the 2005 Doral Open, played on the "Blue Monster" course in a suburb of Miami. Tiger went into the final round two strokes behind Phil Mickelson, one of Tiger's biggest rivals. Tiger birdied the fifth hole to gain a shot, then tied "Lefty"—left-handed Mickelson's nickname—when he birdied the 10th. On the par-5 12th hole, Tiger's clutch 25-foot eagle putt put him in the lead by two strokes.

Mickelson didn't go away, and Tiger had to hold him off with a pressure-packed par putt on the final hole. "You could hear Phil's fans, you could hear [my] fans," an exhausted, but pumped-up, Tiger told

Tiger and Phil Mickelson are the two most popular players in golf. They went head-to-head at the Doral Open in 2005.

Doing Good Off the Course

Tiger Woods is having a huge impact off the golf course, too. In 1996, the same year he turned pro, he and his father Earl established the Tiger Woods Foundation. The Foundation began by setting up special projects for kids, including dozens of golf clinics around the country that teach kids how to play the game, and providing financial grants to youth charities. Since then, it has added a college scholarship program, the Tiger Jam annual fund-raising concert, and Start Something, which encourages kids to set personal goals in education, volunteer activities, and career development. In 2006, the Foundation opened the Tiger Woods Learning Center, a high-tech educational facility, in Anaheim, California. The Center runs after-school classes where kids learn to design their own Web sites, make videos, build a robot, create a comic strip, put on a play, and other valuable lessons.

reporters afterward. "They were both yelling at the top of their lungs." Tiger's 66 for the day gave him a tournament-record, 24-under par total of 264.

Tiger may seem like Superman on the golf course, but he has suffered his share of defeats, as well as a few slumps, as the media likes to call long stretches between wins—especially in majors. Some wondered if he'd lost his desire during a nearly three-year majors drought, from the 2002 U.S. Open to the '05 Masters. Was his marriage to model Swedish model Elin Nordegren in October 2004 a distraction? Tiger's win at the British Open later that summer quieted the doubters.

Then tragedy struck. Earl Woods lost a long battle with prostate cancer on May 3, 2006. A sad Tiger took nine weeks off from the PGA Tour. Still with a heavy heart at the British Open in July, Tiger played four superb rounds and dedicated his win to Earl in a tearful press conference.

There's no telling how many trophies Tiger will own before his career is over.

To highlight that emotional year, in which he won eight of the 15 tournaments he entered—including six in a row—Tiger made it an even dozen majors with the PGA Championship title in August. He was named the Associated Press' Male Athlete of the Year for the fourth time.

At the end of his 11th full season on the PGA Tour in 2007, Tiger was ranked the No. 1 player in the world. Only 31, he stood well on his way to someday being considered the No. 1 golfer of all time.

Tiger Woods' Career Statistics*

Season	Events	CM	W	2	3	T-10	Best	Earnings	Rank	Avg
1996	8	8	2	0	2	5	1	$ 790,594	24	68.4
1997	21	20	4	1	1	9	1	$ 2,066,833	1	69.1
1998	20	19	1	2	2	13	1	$ 1,841,117	4	69.2
1999	21	21	8	1	2	16	1	$ 6,616,585	1	68.4
2000	20	20	9	4	1	17	1	$ 9,188,321	1	67.8
2001	19	19	5	0	1	9	1	$ 5,687,777	1	68.8
2002	18	18	5	2	2	13	1	$ 6,912,625	1	68.6
2003	18	18	5	2	0	12	1	$ 6,673,413	2	68.4
2004	19	19	1	3	3	14	1	$ 5,365,472	4	69.0
2005	21	19	6	4	2	13	1	$ 10,628,024	1	68.7
2006	15	14	8	1	1	11	1	$ 9,941,563	1	68.1
2007	16	26	7	3	0	12	1	$10,867,052	1	67.8
Career	230	216	61	23	17	144	1	$76,579,376	—	—

LEGEND: EVENTS: tournaments entered; CM: cuts made; W: tournament wins: 2: second-place finishes; 3: third-place finishes; T-10: number of top-10 finishes; BEST: best finish in any tournament during that season; EARNINGS: dollar total of prize money won; RANK: ranking on the PGA Tour money list; AVG: per-round scoring average for the season.

* since he turned pro in 1996

GLOSSARY

amateur a person who is not paid to do a job or play a sport

ancient having existed many years; old

diverse ethnicity having ancestors who came from a variety of places around the world

links another name for a golf course

pastime a fun or pleasant way to spend time

phenomenon someone exceptional

prestigious important, or renowned; famous

professional a person who is paid to do a job or play a sport

signature it usually means signing your name; in this case, though, it means a unique or identifying characteristic

sudden-death playoff in golf, a playoff in which the winner is the first player with a better score on a single hole

BOOKS

How I Play Golf
By Tiger Woods
New York, New York: Grand Central Publishing, 2001.
The man himself gives tips and advice for players of all ages and abilities.

KISS Guide to Playing Golf
By Steve Duno
New York, New York: DK Publishing, 2000.
A comprehensive how-to guide to playing golf from the creators of the "Keep It Simple Series."

Michelle Wie (World's Great Athletes)
By Jim Gigliotti
Chanhassen, Minnesota: The Child's World, 2006.
Some experts believe that this teen star may one day challenge Annika Sorenstam's supremacy among female golfers.

Start Something: You Can Make a Difference
By Earl Woods and the Tiger Woods Foundation
New York, New York: Simon & Schuster, 2006.
"Pop," as Tiger called his late father, helped his son start the Foundation. This book tells kids about the TWF's goal of making the world a better place.

WEB SITES

Visit our Web page for lots of links about Tiger Woods:
www.childsworld.com/links

Note to Parents, Teachers, and Librarians: We routinely check our Web links to make sure they're safe, active sites—so encourage your readers to check them out!

INDEX

ABOUT THE AUTHOR

Bob Woods (no relation to Tiger) has written dozens of books and articles on sports for young readers, including a biography of top woman golfer Annika Sorenstam for the WGA series. Bob has also written about NASCAR, motorcycles, football, baseball, and even the movies! He lives in Connecticut.